Animal World

Animal
Patterns

Patricia Whitehouse

www.raintreepublishers.co.uk
Visit our website to find out more information about **Raintree** books.

To order:
☎ Phone 44 (0) 1865 888112
🖹 Send a fax to 44 (0) 1865 314091
💻 Visit the Raintree Bookshop at **raintreepublishers.co.uk** to browse our catalogue and order online.

First published in Great Britain by Raintree, Halley Court, Jordan Hill, Oxford OX2 8EJ, part of Harcourt Education.
Raintree is a registered trademark of Harcourt Education Ltd.

Editorial: Nick Hunter and Diyan Leake
Design: Sue Emerson (HL-US) and Michelle Lisseter
Picture Research: Amor Montes de Oca (HL-US) and Maria Joannou
Production: Lorraine Hicks

Originated by Dot Gradations
Printed and bound in China by South China Printing Company

ISBN 1 844 21537 7 (hardback)
07 06 05 04 03
10 9 8 7 6 5 4 3 2 1

ISBN 1 844 21542 3 (paperback)
07 06 05 04 03
10 9 8 7 6 5 4 3 2 1

British Library Cataloguing in Publication Data
Whitehouse, Patricia
Animal Patterns
516.1'5
A full catalogue record for this book is available from the British Library.

Acknowledgements
The publishers would like to thank the following for permission to reproduce photographs: Alan Paterson p. **4**; Cathy and Gordon ILLG pp. **22**, **24**; Cincinnati Zoo/Ron Austing p. **13**, back cover (cheetah); Corbis pp. **5** (Frank Lane Picture Agency), **11** (W. Wayne Lockwood, M.D.), **18** (Kennan Ward), **19** (Papilio), back cover (toucan, Frank Lane Picture Agency); Eda Rogers p. **9**; FLPA p. **23** (Winifred Wisniewski); Paul Souders pp. **16**, **17**; PhotoDisc pp. **6**, **8**, **10**, **12**; Stock Photography pp. **14** (Jim Gray), **15** (Jim Gray), **20** (Anthony Mercieca/ Photophile), **21** (Anthony Mercieca/Photophile); Tom Stack & Associates p. **7** (Mark Allen Stack)

Cover photograph of zebra pattern, reproduced with permission of PhotoDisc

Contents

What makes a pattern?

Patterns are shapes and colours that repeat.

This zebra crossing is a pattern on the road.

There are patterns on animals, too.

This toucan has stripes on its beak.

What pattern does a zebra have?

This is the pattern on a zebra.

It has black and white stripes.

A zebra looks like a horse
with stripes.

What pattern does a tiger have?

This is the pattern on a tiger.

It has black stripes on its gold hair.

A tiger looks like a big cat
with stripes.

What pattern does a giraffe have?

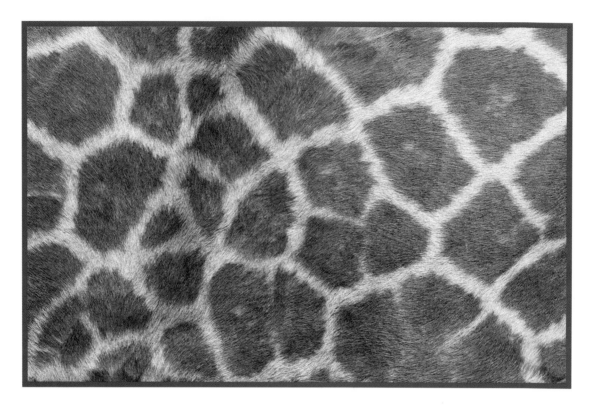

This is the pattern on a giraffe.

It has dark brown spots on light brown fur.

The spots go all the way up the giraffe's long neck.

What pattern does a cheetah have?

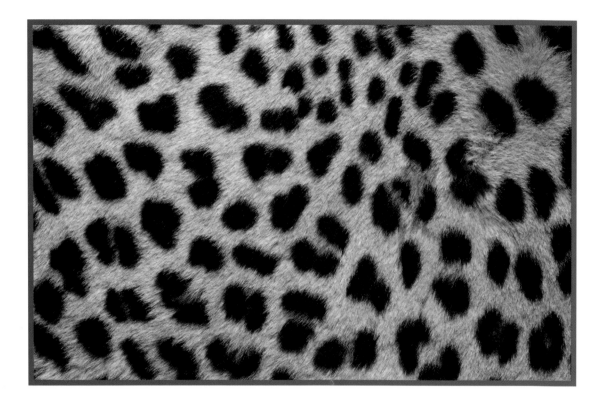

This is the pattern on a cheetah.

It has black spots on its yellow fur.

A cheetah looks like a big spotted cat.

What pattern does a jaguar have?

This is the pattern on a jaguar.

It has black circles on light brown fur.

A jaguar looks like a big cat with a circle pattern on it.

What pattern does a hyena have?

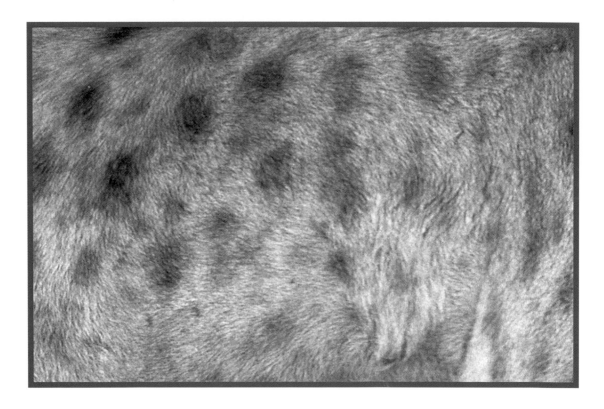

This is the pattern on a hyena.

It has brown spots on its brown fur.

A hyena looks a bit like a
spotted dog.

What pattern does a gila monster have?

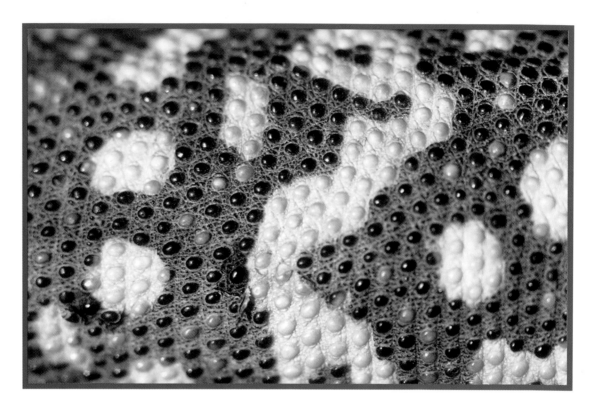

This is the pattern on a gila monster.

(We say, *heela monster*.)

A gila monster has spots and stripes.

It has spots on its back and stripes on its tail.

What pattern does a rattlesnake have?

This is the pattern on a rattlesnake.

It has diamond shapes on its skin.

The pattern goes from its head
to its tail.

What pattern does a peacock have?

This is the pattern on a peacock's tail.

The pattern looks like lots of eyes.

A peacock can show off its great big tail.

Index

Titles in the Animal World series include:

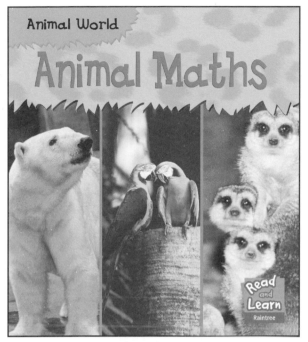

Hardback   1 844 21535 0

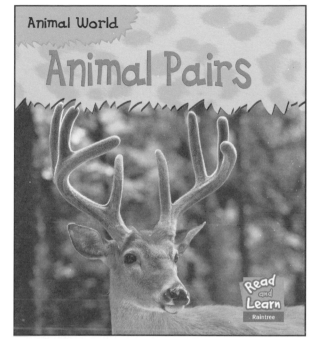

Hardback   1 844 21536 9

Hardback   1 844 21537 7

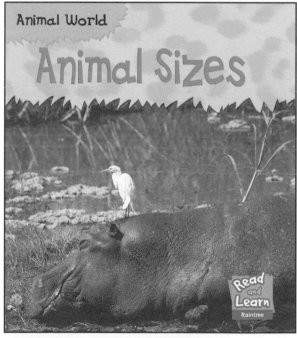

Hardback   1 844 21538 5

Find out about the other titles in this series on our website www.heinemann.co.uk/library